OPTAVIA DIET

- Made Easy -

A Complete Guide To Six-Small-Meals Per Day Philosophy. The 5&1 Medifast Fueling Plan For Weight Loss And Weight Maintenance

By **Diana M. Ramos**

The information provided herein is stated to be truthful and consistent, in that any liability, in terms of inattention or otherwise, by any usage or abuse of any policies, processes, or directions contained within is the solitary and utter responsibility of the recipient reader. Under no circumstances will any legal responsibility or blame be held against the publisher for any reparation, damages, or monetary loss due to the information herein, either directly or indirectly.

Respective authors own all copyrights not held by the publisher.

The information herein is offered for informational purposes solely and is universal as so. The presentation of the information is without contract or any type of guarantee assurance.

About the Author

Diana M. Ramos

"Most people believe that there is a magic formula for weight loss. There is no such thing. But I believe that the real magic is in perseverance and love for one's body. Our only companion on a journey called: life ".

Diana M. Ramos was born near San Antonio and from the early years she had an unconditional passion for cooking.

She has been studying in the field of nutritional science for years with the aim of helping people get better physical shape.

She opened a private practice in 2018 and started following his first clients.

She reached the pinnacle of her success when in 2019 she dedicated her mind and body to finding an easy, fast and inexpensive solution. This solution is the Optavia diet. To date, she follows more than 897 customers who want to lose weight or have an innovative approach to nutrition. His "5 & 1 Meal Plan" is really popular and for this reason she has chosen to write books about her method to help anyone get great results.

Table of Contents

Introduction

In recent years, among the dozens of diet plans out there, a newer, more interesting approach has been receiving the attention of many people as a systematic road to weight loss. And It's called the Optavia Diet. Many well-known names have appreciated the plan, which determines how as to how many meals you should consume per day while also offering those pre-packaged meals.

As foreign as it may sound, the Optavia diet is not a newbie at all. It has a parent diet called "The Medifast Diet," which has its main argument is that it was formulated by physicians. The Medifast Diet may be recalled by some individuals who have always been interested in trying new diets available in the market. Hence, the Optavia Diet is simply a redesign of that, except with some changes in it for better.

Before you dive into the book, let's give you a quick overview of the Optavia Diet. There are three distinct diet plans that people who choose to adopt the Optavia diet program can select from. The variations differ in how many meals you will consume in a day and how many of them are pre-packaged as well as prepared by you at home. Consistent and reliable digital support is, hands down, one of the best things this program offers. In addition to the prepared meals, there are mentors, online help, and guidelines that gradually encourage the change of one habit at a time. Finally, the brand also offers services targeted at seniors and teens. If rapid weight loss is what you want, Optavia Diet could be a remedy. This is most definitely the explanation of why it has gained so much momentum recently. Since the bulk of meals and snacks are pre-made, the diet can also seem smoother and more feasible. In addition to rapid weight reduction, the diet removes alcohol and sugar products, which, when taken in bulk, have clear links to chronic diseases. Desserts, including cookies, as well as most solid fats, like butter and coconut oil, are often prohibited. Finally, the program includes online access, weekly support sessions, and coaching for their online community. This may be an important aspect of progress in weight loss for many people.

In this book, we'll talk about everything you need to know about Optavia Diet. We'll start off with a comprehensive introduction of what portion control really is and how six small frequent meals tend to achieve the goals of portion control and hence, weight loss. We'll talk about the very many benefits of controlling your portions and why is it one of the most, if not the most, important habits you can develop to achieve and maintain a healthy weight loss. We'll also touch upon the issue of the biggest problem that every overweight person faces, i.e., emotional or comfort eating. Afterward, to help you adopt the six-small-meals lifestyle, a section is included on helpful tips to efficiently execute portion control.

After that, we'll introduce the Optavia Diet, its different plans, working principles underneath the program, the foods that are allowed, and the foods you should avoid, along with the benefits and possible risks of following this diet program.

One chapter is dedicated to the 5 & 1 plan for weight loss. It entails the six-step process towards optimal weight along with details on extras like snacks and condiments that you can eat. Furthermore, one chapter is dedicated to the Lean & Green Meals, where we'll discuss the protein and carb components of these meals. There is a sample meal plan for 1200 up to 2200 calories. There is also dining out guide for different cuisines.

Lastly, the final chapter is on transition and the 3 & 3 Plan, where we'll discuss the 3-step process, a sample meal plan, your 4-week journey of habits, and talk about your 3 & 3 Fuelings.

Chap 1: The Six-Meal Per Day Philosophy – Understanding Portion Control

Before we dive into the lengthy details of what Optavia Diet really is and how it works, it is very important to first grasp the whole idea of portion control and how six small frequent meals philosophy achieves that to lose weight. That is why this first chapter is a comprehensive introduction to the idea of eating smaller meals more frequently throughout the day. We'll start off by introducing the concept of portion control. This would be a great start for people who have ever heard of t or never practiced this method to healthy eating and losing weight. Then, we'll get into the significance of it in our daily lives, i.e., why to practice it and what happens if we don't. After that, a section is a dedication to the very many benefits of controlling and limiting our food portions, along with the reasoning and principles behind the efficacy of six small meals per day. Towards the end, we'll touch upon a very important issue of emotional eating (also known as comfort eating). We'll discuss what it is and what are the different ways to actually practice it efficiently in order to shed pounds and be healthier. Finally, the very last section will entail some valuable and easy-to-follow tips and tricks to practice portion control for all of you who struggle with the issue.

1.1 What Is Portion Control?

Are you having difficulty reducing weight? Even if you make healthy lifestyle decisions like denying candy, exchanging French fries with a Caesar salad, and sweating crazy during the workouts? Do you keep on mounting the scale, week in and week out, only to see the same persistent figure looking back at you?

The issue may not be what you consume, but how much you consume. In reality, portion management is always the most difficult challenge on the road to weight reduction for an individual. If you're looking to reduce, increase, or sustain your weight, maintaining fitness is not only about consuming the right foods, it's also about having the correct amount of food. This is actually what management of portions is, not eating more (or even less) calories than the body wants. For weight reduction to take effect, one of the very first items discussed in food planning must be portion control.

Portion control is a means of regulating one's consumption by deciding the number of calories in every food serving and restricting intake to a drop below a defined level.

The secret to effective weight loss is portion control. Regulation of portions of food doesn't simply involve having less food, contrary to common opinion, but rather it implies gaining an understanding of how much you consume and the nutrient content of the food. Sticking to one size at a time lets you maintain a balanced nutrient intake from all the various types of foods. Portion control will also help you restrict empty calories while dining out at a meal or a party, making space for more healthy options in your day.

In addition to ensuring that you make clean food decisions, portion regulation is often the foundation of a proper diet.

Far too much, without caring about the number of calories we intake, we prefer to eat whatever may be set out on the table in front of us. Loneliness, or intense feelings such as elation or profound sadness, may contribute to bingeing. It may also result by being confronted with a wide variety of food options. Controlling one's food intake becomes crucial in view of these factors. The emergence of multiple chronic disorders such as diabetes mellitus, hypertension, excess weight, and unexplained weight loss may be warded off and managed by sufficient but not unnecessary feeding.

The terms "portion" and "serving" are sometimes used interchangeably by individuals, but servings and portions are not exactly the same amount. And if you are monitoring your calorie consumption and learning food labeling, it counts.

A portion is any quantity of a single food that you chose to place on your plate, while a serving is a prescribed volume of such food based on guidelines on health and diet, such as ChooseMyPlate.gov from the US department of agriculture.

Let's look at an instance here. One serving of the cereal and grain category is equivalent to one ounce, as per the agriculture department. Not that much. One ounce of white cooked rice is just half a cup or so. The amount of rice you place on your plate might be a lot greater because you may assume you're just consuming one serving of rice while you really consume two or three servings. That's because a half-cup of rice gives your meal about 100 calories, so you may believe you're just consuming 100 calories, but you're really consuming 200 or 300. You will see how the kcal will rapidly add up.

Mixing up portions and servings may create confusion, especially when you consume energy-dense foods and high-calorie treats, which can contribute to eating extra calories.

The reference of food portion sizes to ordinary items is a simple way to exercise portion management. For starters, according to the National Institution of

Health, a serving of jacket potato is the width of the fist, and one serving of peanut butter is the width of a Ping-Pong ball.

The more calories you're served, the more you're going to consume, as per the Centers for Disease Control and Prevention. So, turn to smaller dishware as you adapt to consuming smaller servings, which again will render your meals look bigger (and anyway, you feed first with your eyes, right?). This is a minor adjustment that will render the task a little less overwhelming.

Simply equate the serving amounts of items to common objects, instead of having to remember charts of teaspoons, cups, and ounces. A single serving of different foods as compared to regular objects are the following:

- Fruit and vegetables are around the size of your palm.

- Pasta is around the size of a single ice cream scoop.

- Beef, fish, or poultry should be the size of a card deck or the size of your palms (excluding the fingers).

- Snacks such as nachos or pretzels are around the equivalent of cupped nachos.

- Peach is equivalent to the size of a baseball.

- The potato is the equivalent of a mouse of a computer.

- Bagel is compared to the size of a hockey puck.

- A doughnut is compared to the width of a CD.

- Boiled rice should be the width of the wrapping of a cupcake.

- Cheese is the size of your entire thumb (from top to bottom) or the size of a couple of dices.

1.2 Significance Of Portion Control

Consuming reasonable quantities is as essential as eating the best ingredients, whether you choose to shed a few kilograms or simply sustain a healthier weight. Food portions of America's restaurants have multiplied or tripled during the past 20 years, as per the National Institution of Health. This disturbing figure strongly leads to the growth in youth and adult rates of obesity. Many Americans have a tough time understanding appropriate quantities and portion sizes for all the super-sized portions they are delivered.

You come to know that it really comes down to ensuring that you have enough fuel for your aspirations as you finally start to comprehend nutrition but still ensuring that you get the proper amount of micro and macronutrients. Now, it's a complicated business to really quantify these criteria, but fortunately, you don't really need to figure out these percentages. You know, human beings lived and prospered long before we were even able to count. It is, therefore, really simple for most species to be relatively healthy and follow a lifestyle that suits their needs. But now it can't be so complicated to do the very same thing, right? Well, actually, this is obviously a yes and no kind of question, as with most stuff. Yes, without needing to worry a lot about it, we can surely have a little problem consuming a well-balanced diet, but also no, in that so long as we exist today in world abundance. For certain reasons, this is wonderful (food shortage doesn't feel like a lot of good), but it ensures it's challenging to eat well but also not eat too well. Now, with the general attitude to dieting, you can overcome this by using a touch of common sense.

Regulation of portions is essential because it enables you to get a tight grip on how much energy you are going to eat. This way, rather than brainlessly bingeing, you are getting what the body wants. Larger portions, clearly, contain more calories. Yet they often inspire persons to consume more than they would normally and to disregard how much calories they really need.

Research from Cornell University showed that 92 percent of anything people place on their plates is consumed by the typical US citizen. As a common concept, we consume it if we see it. So most people, regardless of whether they're consuming or how hungry they actually are, are more inclined to wipe their dishes than leave food unfinished. When eating out, this behavior is especially troublesome, as restaurant-sized meals usually greatly outweigh the quantity of food we really require.

Yet we usually excessively-serve ourselves even at home and hold food in reach, which compels us to consume more. We still appear to feed when distracted, i.e., by the Television, our smartphone, or tablet, to exacerbate the issue, so that we don't know we've had plenty until we reach the bottom of the cookie tin or our spoons come up empty.

1.3 Benefits Of Portion Control

The principles of eating are very easy when it comes to losing weight or just balanced eating in general: don't overeat, monitor your serving sizes, and listen to the fullness of your body. But learning the rules and putting them into effect are two separate things, and the latter can be much harder, particularly when you are looking down at an extra-large bar of chocolate.

However, managing your food portions isn't all lip service; when it comes to scaling back the sum you're putting on your plate, there are some tangible advantages, both physically and economically.

1. Effective Blood Sugar Control

The human body changes the foods we eat into glucose, a form of sugar that serves as the first energy supply for your body, particularly carbohydrates. Your blood sugars rise rapidly after you consume a significant quantity of food. Your pancreas produces insulin whenever the system is overwhelmed with sugar to transfer the glucose into the cells to be used.

So the higher the levels of glucose increase, the more likely the pancreas is to generate far too much insulin in reaction, resulting in low blood sugar levels. As a consequence, your subconscious is fooled into believing that you do need more fuel, and you tend to feel starving, however, with a sugar addiction. By consuming tiny, regular meals, you will stop this negative pattern of low and high blood sugar that can contribute to weight gain, which can help maintain the amount of insulin and glucose steady.

Daily overeating can cause your blood glucose levels to be severely misbalanced. The more you consume, the higher the volume of sugar your body receives. This leads to unsafe jumps in levels and inevitably to diabetes, low blood sugar, etc.

2. Enhanced Satiety And Weight Management

Consuming smaller servings will mitigate the desire to eat and help decrease calorie consumption overall. Feeling satisfied, or feeling complete, will impact how much you consume and how frequently you eat. In order to be more relaxed during a meal, the British Diet Foundation recommends feeding steadily and in smaller servings. Consuming smaller meals often helps the liver, instead of retaining extra fat, to use the nutrition you consume directly as fuel. Losing weight is not as easy as watching the portion sizes, but you will actually practice conscientious eating as you begin to monitor the amount of food you consume, which will help you make better food decisions, as per Harvard Health Publishing. For weight reduction, consuming fewer servings can aid.

To better cut calories and lose excess pounds, pick nutritious meals of appropriate serving sizes.

3. Improved Digestion

All of us were there: the moment when Christmas dinner is finished, and you immediately regret consuming as much as you did. It may not be a huge deal once a year, but consuming large meals daily may cause mayhem in the gastrointestinal tract. Too much food at once only leads to nausea and digestive problems. When it is not filled with food, the digestive system works better. After feeding, monitoring servings can help to avoid stomach cramps and indigestion.

Experts believe that when you consume too much, a few problems happen. It helps the stomach expand more with bigger serving sizes, which allows it to press into the other organs, which may contribute to a lot of pain. You often run the possibility of heartburn, since hydrochloric acid will be forced back into your esophagus from getting a full stomach. Finally, from the huge meal, you may indeed generate excess gas, which is never a pleasant feeling.

It will leave you feeling fatigued and bloated from overeating by overloading your bloodstream with significant portions. Eating fewer meals during the day offers a break from your meals with the digestive system, adjusts the blood glucose levels, and leaves the body feeling healthy.

4. Saving Money

Eating smaller meals, particularly when it comes to eating out, may also lead to significant financial benefits. For instance, ordering kid-sized portions, which are usually less costly than adult meal options and equivalent to the right serving size you can consume, is one way to exercise portion control at diners.

At restaurants, adult food portions may correspond to two, three, or maybe more servings. So, here's a pro tip: Ask your waiter for a take-away box when the food is brought to your table and eliminate at least 50 percent the meal from your dish instantly. By bringing home fifty percent of your purchase, you'll get two servings for the cost of one.

You really don't have to expend a lot on groceries because you consume the suggested portion sizes. Measuring portion amounts can allow the trail mix or nuts packet to last further than eating out of the bag directly.

Sometimes, maintaining a healthier diet is thought impractical since fresh options are pricey, but you can waste less money on food if you take care of your servings. You may also plan your menus for the whole week, reduce the wasting of food, and help you adhere to the amounts you like. Making sure your meal contains a decent balance of protein, fat, and carbohydrates to help keep you happy all day long. Using something would help you stick to your schedule and prevent you from consuming as much as you go out.

5. Helps Control Binge Eating

In certain instances, excessive consumption contributes to bingeing. You render the stomach narrower by practicing portion regulation, which makes you decrease the desire for calories. This, if you have it, will progressively remove the pattern of binge eating.

1.4 How Small Frequent Meals Help With Weight Loss?

The long-held 'three full meals a day' mindset of Americans towards food sometimes means individuals consume a lot in one go. We enjoy the massive portions. So, we always consume more than we should and much more than we should because we have that much food in front of us at a point,

setting us up for short-term bloating and food comas and long-term weight gain. Plus, our blood sugar decreases as we consume a whole day's amount of calories in only a few sessions and go through long stretches of time between feeding, making us exhausted and more prone to look through (and too many) unhealthy things.

That's exactly where it comes in extra handy to 'graze' or consume a lot of micro-meals throughout the whole day instead of a few large ones. Grazers substitute breakfast, lunch, and dinner for six nutritious snacks during the day (or lunch, dinner, and late-night snack foods). For instance, rather than three 660-ish calorie meals, anyone consuming around 2,000 calories a day will nibble on six 330-ish calorie bites.

It's possible that when you think of having to diet to drop fat, you think of fewer snacks, not more. The trouble with restricting yourself to consuming fewer meals a day is that around the middle of each day, you become excessively hungry, and then all options are off. It may seem counterintuitive to eat six days a day, but it's a plan that Harvard Health reports functions for very many individuals. Having six times a day is a simple way to remain full and happy during the day, as long as your portions are tiny and only half the energy of full-size portions, meaning you're less prone to eat at night. And if the newspaper you encounter in the bathroom at work is your primary source of knowledge, you've definitely learned you ought to consume more than six balanced meals a day to reduce weight. This technique allows your body to exhaust calories continuously and makes sure you're still satisfied and never starving. The way our predecessors consumed is similar: by tossing food into their rugged mouths when they hunted or gathered it. You should not eat six enormous portions a day, though. For meals, keep the size of your two fists for meals and adhere to palm-sized portions for snacks. Conversely, you should have all the meals about the same size or less. Having all serving sizes the same assures your system that there is plenty of food and that no fat needs to be processed.

Your metabolic rate, mental and physical energy levels, performance, temperament, and appetite will be greatly influenced by feeding more often. What you're consuming counts, of course. Do everything right, and you will find that consuming smaller frequent meals is the brain and body-boosting habit adjustment you will need to lose weight effectively.

One research released in the Journal of the Academy of Nutrition and Dietetics showed that people who consumed small, more regular meals consumed fewer calories in general, had lower BMIs, and were more likely than those who ate less, larger meals to eat healthier foods.

Eventually, you will often feel healthier when feeding more often. How? When you go hours without feeding, the decreases in blood sugar that result signal the cells release stress-related chemicals, including cortisol and epinephrine (i.e., adrenaline), which may lead to difficulties with sleep and attitude.

The better these chemicals are in balance, the more probable you are to be rejuvenated through the day and to be able to relax well enough at night. Plus, feeding also delivers a constant supply of glucose to the brain, helping to improve cognitive function and efficiency. These are all the positive stuff about both your professional life and your private life.

Rather than 2 to 3 big ones, several sustainable nutrition plans recommend consuming 5 or 6 smaller meals a day. That seems like a lot to certain people, and others may also disregard this suggestion as they want to lose weight. Many individuals have been advised all their adult years that weight reduction is a straightforward calorie-in, calorie-out equation. So, they presume the fewer calories they eat, the more fat they're likely to lose. People make many mistakes in an effort to gain as little caloric intake as needed in the span of any day. Before lunch, they tend not to consume something. Then, after 7:00 p.m., they don't eat anymore. The bulk of them wind up just consuming two actual meals a day.

The irony is that these 'techniques' for weight management are bringing us more damage than benefit. They play with your plans for weight reduction and even your gut health. Let's take a peek at some of the explanations why it is healthier to consume 5 to 6 smaller meals every day!

1) Helps Control Appetite

A big trick to maintaining track of your appetite is to consume 5 or 6 smaller meals every day, around 3 hours apart. At those tiny meals, if you consume nutritious whole foods, such as lean meat (meat, milk, and starches), fibrous vegetables and fruits, and slow-burning unrefined carbs (such as whole grains rather than processed white sugar and flour), you can remain full during the day, and you would be less prone to encounter sugar cravings and splurges. Alternatively, you can feel too ravenous if you feed just twice a day that you over-consume (or eat fewer nutritious foods) and wind up consuming more food than you will on a five or 6-times-a-day diet schedule.

2) Maintains Good Energy Levels

You have undoubtedly encountered the mid-morning crash that can drive all of us to the snack machine or the lunchroom at work searching for nourishment (mostly in the form of carbohydrates) if you have ever consumed just caffeine and a croissant for breakfast. Similarly, if you don't consume a lot all day long and then consume a major lunch, there's a second drop in the afternoon that hits, forcing us to crawl our way to McDonald's on our early lunch. Eating very seldom will cause big blood sugar spikes and drops. However, eating tiny, frequent meals 5 or 6 times a day maintains the blood glucose levels stable. During the day, this will help control your stress levels and help prevent you from giving in to sugar cravings.

3) Boosts Metabolism

Perhaps the easiest reason to consume quick, healthy meals would be the help with losing weight. More often, feeding helps improve the metabolic rate and prevents it from initiating the reaction to hunger mode. Your body's natural response is to slow its energy expenditure to save resources if you do go without food for many hours on end. That is true! Eating seldom causes you to slow down your metabolism. This is why, as quickly and easily as possible after waking up, the Optavia Diet plan also suggests consuming breakfast, as well as a little bit before bed. Because it is a long period of time for your system to go without energy intake for those 8 hours you're sleeping, it is necessary to eat both before sleep and then when you wake up to prevent the metabolic rate from entering starving mode.

4) Keeps Hormones In Balance

In the human body, there are many endocrine hormones that impact levels of appetite, metabolic rate, and weight management. Let's have a peek at two of them: ghrelin and insulin. When we actually feed, a decreased meal rate triggers a greater insulin response. It has two nasty consequences here. The spikes turn on pathways that enhance fat accumulation, first of all. Secondly, crashes that lead us to feel heavy food cravings and desire candy also accompany the peaks. This is a horrific double-edged weight loss sword! Making it worse, for several hours at a time, the lack of meal in the stomach allows the gut to secrete ghrelin, commonly known as the 'hormone of hunger.' Ghrelin shuts down the processing of fat and raises appetite. When the body is deprived for long amounts of time, our temptation to consume rises and drives us to consume more in one meal than we actually need; in the quest to lose weight, you can actually begin to understand how so many of these bodily functions can add up to build a complete halt.

5) Digestion Improves

Consuming tiny, regular meals scattered during the day often impacts our well-being greatly. When we place small, accessible volumes of food in the body little by little instead of a large food explosion twice a day, it makes us eat faster. When we consume tiny doses more often, it is simpler for our intestines to process and digest minerals and vitamins from our diets. In reality, to support people with stomach problems, including acid reflux, many physicians prescribe consuming smaller portions more often. Consuming tiny, regular meals is an essential component for good wellness and weight loss targets. The most significant thing, though, is what you consume at such meals.

Things To Remember

First and foremost, what you consume is incredibly significant, regardless of what you snack. You lose out on the amount of nutrition, fat, and protein your body requires when you graze on processed or sugary foods, and undergo the glucose levels spike and fall that is supposed to discourage grazing, says Jones. Avoid fried grains with white flour or artificial sugar, and combine carbohydrates with protein and healthier fats in order to be as blood-sugar-friendly as possible.

When you concentrate a little more on the wall clock than your internal clock, feeding can also go haywire. You will quickly get out of sync with your own appetite signals and wind up getting into a habit of overeating if you convince yourself you ought to feed every three hours or so.

Divide your total calories equally and prepare mini-meals that contain a mix of protein, healthy fats, and complex carbohydrates from whole ingredients such as almonds, fresh fruit, cooked kidney beans, and low-sugar yogurt to maintain your mini-meals in line with your needs. You set yourself up with the correct combination of rejuvenating eating in this manner.

Then, tap into your bodies and then let the grazing be driven by your appetite and satiety thresholds. Consume when you're hungry, but don't wait until you're desperately hungry. You may feel relaxed, but not crazy loaded, in between each micro-meal. Please wait for twenty minutes or so if you're still hunger (or just want to continue feeding), and re-evaluate the messages from your body before doing so.

1.5 How To Tackle Emotional Eating?

We don't eat just to relieve physical hunger. For warmth, stress reduction, or to reward oneself, many of us often turn to food. And we prefer to reach out for fast food, candy, and other soothing yet harmful things when we do. When you feel sad, you may reach for a cup of ice cream, order a pizza if you are bored and lonely, or stop by the drive-through after a long day at work.

Emotional eating involves food to help oneself feel better, rather than the stomach, to meet emotional needs. Comfort eating, sadly, doesn't cure emotional issues. Probably, it generally makes you feel worse. Afterward, the initial mental struggle not only persists, but you feel bad about binge eating as well.

It isn't always a negative thing to sometimes use eating as a pick-me-up, a treat, or to rejoice. But when food is the main emotional coping method, you get trapped in an addictive loop where the actual feeling or concern is never tackled, because your first instinct is to open the fridge anytime you are depressed, frustrated, furious, sad, tired, or bored.

How you consume is just as or even more significant than what you consume. In emotional overeating, the overall amount of food you consume, your disposition toward eating, how you manage your snacks and meals, and your personal food choices may play a far greater role than the actual foods you want to consume. Take time to evaluate your eating habits, understand more about regular eating vs. emotional eating, and build different methods of self-help to resolve both your mental and physical food relationships. Start practicing saying "no," not just to harmful foods, but also to circumstances that undermine your attempts to build healthier dietary patterns that are emotionally mindful.

When you're emotionally at the weakest place, the worst food cravings strike. When experiencing a tough situation, feeling depressed, or even feeling bored, you may look to food for warmth-consciously or subconsciously. Comfort eating will undermine your attempts to lose weight. It also contributes to too much consumption, particularly too much of high-calorie, fatty and sugary desserts. The positive news is that you may take action to retake control of your dietary behaviors and get back on board with your weight reduction plans if you're susceptible to emotional eating.

1. Recognize Addictive Behavior

Study studies have been dedicated to the issue of food addiction for years, whether or not anyone may be addicted to certain foods, specifically those created with processed goods such as white flour, sugar, salt, and fat, and whether, in turn, these foods were accountable for such habits of bingeing and excessive consumption. As it could not be proved that food itself became addictive, scientists started to look at the habits' addictive features. Addiction components include addictive behavior involvement (such as overeating), lack of control, behavioral preoccupation (eating), having only brief gratification, and permanent detrimental effects (becoming unhealthy or obese from overeating).

2. Separate Emotional Signals From Hunger Signals

The distinction between feeding in reaction to appetite and feeding in reaction to emotion may be challenging to perceive and recognize. Through feeding mindfully and paying attention to hunger cues, learn to distinguish the two, and self-regulate your food intake. Practice evaluating your hunger: Exactly how hungry are you on a scale of 1 to 10? If you don't feel hungry or you're only a little hungry, anywhere between one and four, you should rank it. Wait until you hit five, very hungry (but don't let yourself get too hungry to the extent that you overeat.)

3. Develop A Schedule

Eating regularly scheduled meals and scheduled snacks for certain persons, if you keep to the routine, will deter overeating. On the other side, since they lead to random feeding and bingeing, erratic eating patterns typically mean disaster. Generally speaking, at various hours of the day, most people plan three courses and one or two snacks or "micro meals." Typically, true hunger comes in about three hours after the last meal. A tiny snack might be enough at that moment, depending on your eating patterns and the time of day; if not, you get a signal that it's time for your next meal.

4. Change The Patterns Of Eating

Some research has shown that for some individuals, missing food, consuming late at night, and other irregular eating habits may contribute to weight gain. It doesn't imply that as soon as you wake up the next morning, you can or should have breakfast, nor does it imply that you shouldn't consume something at night. However, it might be time to follow a different pattern if eating habits don't help you shed weight or manage over-eating. Short-term research has also shown that consuming the main meal at noon (for lunch) will help to promote weight reduction and weight management rather than later in the day or what might be deemed usual dinner time.

5. Find Different Ways To Satisfy Your Emotions

You would not be able to regulate your food habits for too long if you don't know how to handle your feelings in a manner that doesn't rely on food. Diets too frequently fail because they provide rational dietary guidance that only works if the food patterns are deliberately managed. When feelings derail the system, expecting an instant payoff with food, so it doesn't work.

In order to prevent emotional feeding, you must find other avenues to psychologically satisfy yourself. It's not enough to grasp the emotional eating cycle or even to recognize your causes, even though it's a big first step. For emotional satisfaction, you need substitutes for food that you can resort to.

Several other alternatives to comfort eating are given here:

- Call somebody who always helps you feel good, whether you're sad or lonely, interact with your cat or dog, or glance at a childhood picture or special photo album.

- Release your inner tension if you're restless by listening to your favorite tune, holding a tension ball, or enjoying a fast stroll.

- Give yourself a hot cup of tea if you're tired, take a nap, light some scented candles, or get yourself in a heated blanket.

- Read a good novel, watch a television show, wander in nature, or switch to a hobby that you love (woodworking, guitar playing, playing basketball, jigsaw puzzles, etc.) if you're bored.

6. Get Social Support

If needed, a community of friends and family, including clinical support in the form of a psychologist or mentor, maybe as vital to your progress as your own encouragement and actions. Many that care for your well-being will assist by supporting you, exchanging suggestions for healthy foods, acknowledging the social foundations of your unhealthy eating problems, and maybe even helping to solve any of the mental conditions that affect your emotional eating. Surround yourself with friends who are able to lend an ear, give support and inspiration, or maybe join in as buddies for dining, walking, or exercising.

1.6 Tips To Effectively Practice Portion Control

Here are a few of the tips you can use to practice controlling your portions to lose weight.

1. Measure Portions To Avoid Overeating

Portion regulation helps with an appreciation of serving quantities through consuming only the proper quantity of every food. As a guide, use the "Nutrition Facts" table used on all pre-prepared items. The serving size, accompanied by the number of servings contained in the package, is the first entry. Much of the details below depend on the quantity of food in the single serving, like carbohydrates, fat, and sodium. If you consume double the serving size, you have double the amount of calories, carbohydrates, and fats mentioned. Measure the snack or count the number of cookies where possible, for instance, and be sure you don't consume further than you planned.

You have to weigh them in order to understand the exact portions of food. Measuring containers and bowls can aid, but overfilling a cup or bowl can be simple. Using a modern food scale, the most effective way to calculate meals is by weight.

2. Serve Your Food On A Plate

Placing the meals on a plate instead of consuming out of the tub, jar, or served dish is another perfect way to maintain portion sizes. Fill half of your dish with lettuce and vegetables for dinner and lunch and then split the other half into proteins and carbohydrates. If you have to look for a second portion, you can overeat less frequently.

3. Limit Nibbling On Food While You're Preparing

You ought to give up grazing in order to consume fewer. It's enticing to taste the food while you're preparing, but it's best to wait before the dinner is made. By the same point, it's tempting to neglect to count calories that were not on your own plate, so avoid taking leftovers from the plate of your kid or partner. You will broaden your mind to the excess calories you gain in a day by maintaining a food journal. For a few days, write down any bite you take or drink you sip, and then read the list. The findings may shock you and promote better dietary behaviors.

4. Don't Bring Extra Food Onto The Table

Set aside any food that won't be placed on your plate once you settle down to eat. If you have to pull the food out once again, you would be less motivated for a further serving. Even overeating may be induced by only having food lying inside arms reach. Concealing leftover food, quick snacks, and sweets somewhere you can't see them all the time will help you consume little.

5. Split The Food

Owing to the large serving sizes that restaurants offer, dining out is a significant contributor to bingeing. Try consuming just half the food the next time you head out. You'll conserve half the amount of calories. Through packing up some extra portion of "to go" before you even feed, you may ask your waiter to help. Dividing a meal with a mate is yet another simple — and inexpensive — way to consume less.

6. Include More Veggies

If you are going to overeat something, the safest way is to eat vegetables. Next, load your bowl with veggies with a minimum of five servings of veggies a day are more likely to achieve, and vegetables are very low in fat and calories, but high in fiber as well as other phytonutrients and phytonutrients. That's very effective in helping you preserve good fitness. When it comes to loading the plate, nutritionists advocate concentrating on non-starchy vegetables.

Consume as much Caesar salad as you want to spice up the meal (such as kale, broccoli, tomato, celery, and zucchini). Include herbs for flavor, but retain the prescribed portion size with fat, protein, and carbohydrates. A perfect way to fuel up without eating more calories is to incorporate more veggies into your recipes. Begin your dinner with lettuce, finish your lunch with vegetables and carrots, and add your morning eggs to your preferred steamed veggies.

7. Use Plates That Are Smaller

Over the decades, when plate dimensions have risen, so have food portions. To hold portions in control, pick a 9 "plate for grownups and a 7" plate for kids. Your plate will appear fuller; your subconscious will be fooled into believing that you have more fuel.

8. Always Listen To Your Body

We're all guilty of multitasking. Try to stop feeding when watching Television or while you're on the phone, however. Studies suggest that mindless consumption contributes to excess weight, so make sure to calculate the right portion sizes and actually consume your treats from a bowl.

It sounds so easy, but in reality, many of us let our minds rule our bodies, particularly when it comes to emotional eating, rather than the other way around. Ask yourself whether you're very hungry before getting a snack or whether you're listening to your desires or feeding out of habit. Consume less by not using eating to cope or distract you; instead, take a stroll. And don't just grab a bag of snacks while you're watching a movie or buy popcorn while you're at the cinema.

9. Be Smart About Salads

Thought food portions for salads wouldn't count? Often, remember. It's good to be aware of your chopped vegetables and portions, much as for other meals. For optimum eating and a healthy mix of ingredients, figure out how to make the best of your next salad.

10. Drink Water Before Eating

Do not forget to consume a ton of water prior to eating before you get to sort your meals. One of the easiest strategies is to drink a glass of water half an hour before a meal or whatever you snack. This is because you're more apt to consume extra while you're dehydrated. It ensures you get more water throughout from getting the huge glass of water, but you're still less likely to get that large a portion amount.

11. Use A Plate Or Your Palm As A Guide

Use the plate or palm guideline to get a sense of the quantity of starch, calories, fats, and vegetables to have in a serving. Divide the portion into half a dish of vegetables of low starch, a fifth of a plate of protein, and a fourth of a plate of complex carbohydrates and half a tablespoon of fat. Use the palm to 'measure' out reasonable quantities, and use it in combination with the plate principle.

Note to maintain the size of your hand palm for protein, the tip of your finger as a butter serving size, a fourth of an avocado per serving, and no more than the width of a matchbox to measure cheese.

12. Use the Same Plates and Bowls

Think about it: when it's placed on a large plate, a regular pasta serving seems even smaller, implying that after eating, we're more inclined to feel dissatisfied. Whether the plate is rather big or tiny, or whether the bowls are wider than you've been had before, it's very simple to get a bit confused in your mind. You assume you have the same quantity, however, because of the illusion of the portion you're having more.

13. Change Your Spoon Size

Admit it; you eat more than soup with your oversized spoons. Okay, it's time to quit the trend because evidence suggests that we consume fewer if we use a teaspoon instead of a tablespoon, according to experts. So, if possible, pick a smaller scooper, and specifically when it comes to calorie-rich snacks like ice cream.

Another pro tip: Consider switching the broad serving spoons, too; it's tougher to put on huge quantities with a smaller version.

14. Eat Slowly And Savor

Eating quick ensures you're more apt to skip the indicators of hunger and fullness. Taking the time with a meal, actually treasuring each taste, encourages you to experience the meal further, and can ensure that you don't overeat what you're consuming. This implies not pacing in front of the TV over the countertop or gulping down dinner. Sit and eat mindfully frequently. Eaten quickly and in a rush, food will feel less enjoyable.

Mind to ensure your foods are balanced in terms of macro and micronutrients, a source of nutrition, good fats, and complex carbs, to make these portion-controlled meals more fulfilling. Have low GI carbohydrates such as lentils, chickpeas, beans, brown rice, quinoa, and butternut squash. They're all excellent sources of food you absorb slowly and offer you energy for a long period. Include healthier fats such as avocado, almonds, nuts, and olive oil because the fat makes us remain fuller, plus it's very nice for your skin, hair, and body. And, of course, high-quality poultry, such as meat, sustainably captured salmon and leaner varieties of grass-fed beef and lamb, if necessary. This aims to enhance the quality of the fatty acids found in the meat. Add more of legumes, tofu, and kimchi for vegetarian forms of protein. Not only is stuff like lentils (chickpeas, lentils) a decent supply of carbs, they add up and are also a very nice source of protein.

Chapter 2: Introducing Optavia Diet

In this chapter, we'll talk everything about the Optavia diet from the basics of what it is, how it works, what foods are allowed, and prohibited to benefits and potential risks of the program.

2.1 What Is Optavia Diet?

As the term itself hasn't been in the public eye for long, the Optavia Diet could sound foreign. You're more inclined to have learned of the diet that was renamed as Optavia in mid-2017. Its former name was "Take Shape For Life."

Take Form for Life launched as an affiliate of the weight reduction products company Medifast, established in 1980 by Dr. William Vitale, a medical practitioner. The goal of "Take Shape for Life" was to sell Medifast's goods in an online environment best tailored to the modern era when it was launched in 2002.

You may be drawn to a diet that significantly reduces your time in the kitchen when you don't like cooking or don't have time to prepare meals. The Optavia diet does exactly that. It supports weight reduction by a blend of low-calorie, pre-packaged foods, a few quick home-cooked recipes, and a coach's one-on-one help.

The Optavia Diet is not meant for a specific community but aims to cater to individuals who choose to avoid "overanalyzing" an eating schedule.

Five out of the six small meals a day are pre-planned and pre-packaged with Optavia's famous '5 & 1' plan, removing the need for any major choices when it's time to feed. Optavia happens to be a choice of individuals with a packed schedule, but the reduced-calorie strategy of the product is meant for anybody who wishes to lose weight.

Medifast, a meal replacement organization, owns the Optavia diet. Optavia and Medifast's main diet consists of low-calorie, low carb plans that blend processed goods with fresh recipes to support weight reduction (also named Medifast). The Optavia diet, though, requires one-on-one coaching, unlike Medifast.

They all include marketed items named Optavia Fuelings, and homemade meals known as Lean and Green meals, and you can pick from many choices. Optavia Fuelings contains over 60 foods that are low in carbohydrates but a good source of protein and probiotic strains that contain helpful bacteria that will improve the health of your intestines. Bars, cakes, mixes, pies, dairy products, sauces, and pastas are there with many more items.

While they can seem to be very high in carbohydrates, they are built to be lower in sugars and carbohydrates than conventional variants of the same items usually have. The organization uses glucose replacements and limited serving sizes to do this. In addition, several products are packaged with whey protein powder and soy-based isolate. The brand has a range of pre-made low-carb foods named Flavors of Home that can supplement Lean and Green meals for those not skilled in cooking.

Versions Of Octavia Diet

Two weight reduction plans and one weight management strategy are used in the Optavia diet:

- Optimal Weight 5&1 Plan. This version contains five Optavia Fuelings, the most common package, and one nutritious Lean and Green meal per day.

- Optimal Weight 4&2&1 Plan. This package provides four Optavia Fuels, two Lean and Green dishes, and one snack a day for those who require additional calories or variety in food choices.

- Optimal Health 3&3 Plan. This one contains three Optavia Fuels and three nutritious Lean and Green meals a day, optimized for maintenance.

Additional resources to promote weight reduction and maintenance are offered by the Optavia community, like tips and encouragement by text message, online groups, weekly phone calls, and an application that helps you to set menu reminders and monitor food intake and exercise.

Specialized services for breastfeeding mothers, elderly adults, teenagers, and individuals with hypertension or gout are often offered by the company. While these tailored plans are supported by Optavia, it is uncertain if this diet is suitable for individuals with certain health issues. In addition, teens and nursing moms have special demands for nutrients and calories that the Optavia diet does not meet.

2.2 How Does It Work?

The Optavia Diet offers users, like most meal-replacement programs, its own variety of packaged items that take over the role of many meals during the day. Optavia includes lifestyle plans with weight reduction and weight management targets. The other plans of Optavia, the "3 & 3" and "4 & 2 & 1", incorporate "real" meals with substitutes for meals. These deals are better for people who choose to steadily reduce weight or sustain their existing weight. Both "fueling" and "lean and green" prepared meals are kept inside tight calorie amounts on all Optavia schedules.

You begin by making a phone call with a trainer, irrespective of the plan you select, to help decide which Optavia plans to pursue, set targets for weight reduction, and acquaint oneself with the system.

The tagline of Optavia is "Lifelong Transition, One Healthy Habit at a Time." The main emphasis of the Optavia diet is a way of eating focused on several mini-meals (called "Fuelings") eaten during the day, complemented by a home-cooked meal (termed "lean and green"). The program is built on six main optimum health building blocks:

- Weight Loss

- Nutrition And Hydration

- Motion

- Sleeping

- Your Mind

- Your Environment

The argument goes that you are less prone to wander into poor eating territories if you have a diet to follow and recommended mini-meals to consume. And weight reduction is almost assured because you just consume the small number of calories that the diet gives, even as little as 1,100 calories a day. In comparison, balanced home cooking becomes a routine every night by planning your own "lean and green" meal, allowing the shift from the program back to "normal" healthier eating smoother.

Optavia also provides the aspect of social support that separates it from several other diets that substitute meals. As social support is a significant factor in the progress of weight reduction, those who participate in their services have access to a mentor, usually someone who has done the plan effectively. For your weight reduction path, this coach will address concerns, offer guidance, and act as a cheerleader.

Beginning Phase

Most people begin with the Optimal Weight 5&1 weight loss program, which is an 800-1,000 calorie routine said to help you lose 12 pounds over 12 weeks (5.4 kg). You consume 5 Optavia Fuelings every day on this menu and 1 Lean and Green meal every day. You're expected to consume one meal every 2-3 hours and, on most days of the week, involve 30 minutes of a moderate workout. In sum, the Fuelings and food focus on providing no more than 100 grams of carbohydrates per day. As Optavia trainers are compensated on commission, you purchase these Fuelings from your trainer's specific page.

The aim of Lean and Green meals is to be rich in proteins and lighter in carbs. One meal contains 5-7 ounces of cooked lean protein (145-200 grams), three pieces of veggies, and up to 2 portions of good fats.

This schedule also involves one extra snack a day, which the coach would authorize. Three veggie sticks, 1/2 cup (60 grams) of sugar-free jelly, or 1/2 ounce (14 grams) of nuts are Plan-approved snacks. A dining-out guide that describes how to eat a Lean and Green meal at any favorite place is also included in the program. Please remember that the 5&1 Program actively prohibits alcohol.

Maintenance Phase

You begin a six-week maintenance period after you hit the target weight, which includes steadily raising calories of not more than 1,550 calories a day and incorporating a wider wide variety of foods, like whole grains, vegetables, and low-fat dairy goods. You are expected to switch over to the Optimal Health 3&3 plan after six weeks, which involves 3 Lean and Green meals and 3 Fuelings every day, plus regular Optavia training. The choice of being qualified as an Optavia trainer is for those who achieve solid results in the process.

Here is a list of items that Optavia Fuelings options consist of:

- Smoothies

- Beef stew

- Shakes

- Snack or meal-replacement bars

- Turkey meatball marinara

- Chicken cacciatore

- Chicken with rice and vegetables

- Smashed potatoes

- Popcorn

- Pancakes

- Rustic tomato herb penne

- Mac and cheese

- Wild rice and chicken soup

- Cookies

- Cereal

The following are all the foods that are allowed to prepare your Lean & Green meals at home. They include:

- Healthy fats (canola oil, avocado, low-carb salad dressing, olive oil, and olives, etc.)

- Shellfish (crab, shrimp, scallops)

- Whole eggs (maximum three per week)

- turkey or Chicken

- Ground meat (at least 85 percent lean)

- Fish (cod, tuna, tilapia, flounder)

- Egg Beaters or Egg whites

- tenderloin or Pork chop

- Game meat (buffalo)

- Tofu

- Lean beef

- Vegetables (leafy greens, radishes, cucumbers, mushrooms, asparagus, and broccoli, etc.)

The diet recommends a reduction in the consumption of caffeinated caffeine or soda after noon per day as it comes to beverages. Instead, to fulfill the hydration needs, it is advised to blend Optavia Purposeful Hydration packs, which include vitamins and antioxidants, into a drink.

A diet program named Medifast entered the market in the '80s with processed weight loss meals. In order to replace lunch and breakfast, those mail-order blends and treats were introduced, rendering weight reduction a no-brainer. While Medifast is still in business today, it has a range of famous branches working under the same premise as pre-selected weight reduction meal replacements. The Optavia diet, which was formerly recognized as Take Shape for Life, is one of them.

With its intense ease, the Optavia diet caters to dieters. (There's really nothing any better than getting your meals delivered to your house, after all.) In particular, the easy-to-follow format takes the trial and error out of meal preparation.

Know Your Optavia Fuelings

The food items from Optavia are Optavia Fuelings. Classic Fuelings, Essential Fuelings, and Select Fuelings are available. All and all, you may pick from over 60 products that provide calories in your journey to reducing weight. The Essential Fuelings includes alternatives:

- Double Chocolate Brownie

- Cheesy Buttermilk Cheddar Mac

- Vanilla Creamy

- Shake of Strawberry

- Silky Peanut Butter with Chocolate Chip Bar and much more.

Optavia Fuelings includes 24 high-quality, full protein, lactic acid bacteria minerals and vitamins, and no artificial colors, flavors, or sweeteners. Optavia Select Fuelings has global-inspired recipes. The brand also employs non-GMO ingredients obtained from all over the world. You will select from 13 bold varieties and foreign flavors such as Bolivian chia seeds, Mediterranean rosemary, and Indonesian cinnamon. Your calorie restriction program would dictate the number of Fuelings that you consume per day.

- Fuel is a ready-made product, so you don't have to make anything at mealtime.

- You will participate and save cash on the goods as a coach and market them to anyone if you like.

- Having 60 or so fuels to pick from implies that you might eventually get tired of having the same food again and again.

- Must buy from a distributor of the company.

They claim items and services have been suggested by and adopted for more than one million people for more than 20,000 clinicians. Nutritious, sweet, and efficient are Optavia Fuelings. At every point of the journey, they are clinically developed to have the best foods and are nutrient-dense, rightly portioned, and nutritionally compatible.

Through Optavia Fuelings, this may happen to many individuals; when you catch yourself losing the weight, make sure to keep it smooth and steady. Dramatic improvements that induce seriously, rapid weight loss are not permanent, because no matter how successful Fuelings can be, they can impact the outcomes if consumed too little. You have to return the meals before 30 days since receiving the order for a complete refund (excluding shipping and handling expenses) if you are not 100 percent happy with your order. All returns include a Return

Authorization Code, collected at 1-888-Optavia from the Client Success Team. Only on consumable goods

and blenders only, refunds are eligible. When you return, put the items in the original packaging. A refund does not apply for any extra promotional products you may have got. The obligation for all returned postage charges is yours.

2.3 What You Can And Cannot Eat

Here are the allowed and non-compliant foods.

Compliant Foods

The bulk of the food you consume on the diet plans of Optavia comes straight from the brand, but you would often need to buy things to make your "lean and green" dish of each day.

1. Optavia "Fuelings."

The bulk of the food you consume on the Optavia Diet would take the shape of the pre-packaged fuels. You will select from over 60 smoothies, bars, drinks, pretzels, and other items (even brownies!) as meal replacements, according to Optavia's online guide. The corporation notes each food has a nutritional profile that is almost similar, which ensures that it is easy to consume them synonymously.

2. Lean Meats

A five-to-seven-ounce amount of prepared lean protein needs to be used in the "lean and green" meals you'll make.

Here's how to pick lean meats. Using the following illustrations, Optavia distinguishes between heavy, leaner, and leanest protein sources:

- Lean: Salmon, lamb, or pork chops

- Leaner: Chicken breast or swordfish

- Leanest: Cod, shrimp, and egg whites

3. Non-Starchy Vegetables and Greens

In your "lean and green" dinner, Optavia's 5 & 1 plan consists of two veggies with the protein. The veggies are split into groups of lower, moderate, and higher carbs, with examples as follows:

- Lower Carb: Greens veggies

- Moderate Carb: Summer squash or cauliflower

- Higher Carb: Peppers or broccoli

4. More Healthy Fats

A "lean and green" dish may be made with up to two portions of good fats, like olive or walnut oil, coconut oil, or avocado, in addition to quality protein and green leafy vegetables.

5. Fresh Fruit, Low-Fat Dairy, And Whole Grains

When the weight reduction that customers expected by food replacements, healthy protein, and non-starchy vegetables has been accomplished, they will continue on to a diet to manage their weight. People can start to incorporate other food groups under Optavia's weight maintenance packages. In the "3 & 3" and "4 & 2 & 1," weight loss plans, low-fat dairy, organic produce, and whole grains are also included.

Foods You Should Avoid

While the plans of Optavia do not ban certain items, they do suggest that you eliminate or reduce your consumption of less nutritious choices that are unlikely to aid your weight reduction and may not have useful nutrients. At first, other foods can be reduced, but eventually brought back as you achieve your targets for weight loss. This involves crops that are starchy, new fruits, nuts, and low-fat dairy.

1. Decadent Desserts

Not unexpectedly, with desserts like cakes, cookies, or ice cream, Optavia prohibits indulging the sugar cravings. Moderate sweet snacks such as fresh fruit or frozen yogurt will find its way into the diet after the original weight loss process, however.

2. High -Calorie Additions

The flavor is added by butter, shortening, and high-fat pasta sauces. However, they add huge quantities of calories as well. You would be recommended to hold additions to a modest or replace lower-calorie variants of Optavia.

3. Sugary Beverages

Sweetened products such as soft drinks, soda, or fruit juices contain calories without any fulfillment, so Optavia's plans are firmly against them.

4. Alcohol

Users are advised to restrict alcohol by the Optavia plan. A 5-ounce glass of wine with 120 calories or

150 calories in a 12-ounce beer may add up rapidly if you're trying to remain within a limited calorie range.

2.4 Benefits And Risks Of Optavia Diet

Benefits Of Optavia Diet

If you want a diet program that is simple and easy to execute, which can help you lose weight easily, and provides built-in support networks, Optavia's plan may be a good match for you.

1. Easy To Follow

Since the diet depends primarily on pre-packaged foods, on the 5&1 plan, you are only accountable for preparing one meal a day. What is more, to make things easy to execute, each schedule arrives with food journals and sample food choices. Although you are expected to prepare 1-3 Lean and Green recipes every day, they are quick to create based on the plan, since the package provides unique recipes and a selection of choices for food. In addition, to supplement lean and green foods, many that are not interested in preparing can purchase prepared meals named "Flavors of Home."

The shakes, soups, and other such meal replacement items from Optavia are shipped straight to your house, a degree of comfort that is not offered by many other diets. While for "lean and green" dishes, you would need to look for your own products, the home delivery alternative for the "Fuelings" of Optavia saves time and effort. They're quick to cook and make great grab-and-go dishes once the package arrives.

2. May Improve Blood Pressure

Via weight loss and decreased sodium intake, Optavia plans may help improve blood pressure. Although the Optavia diet has not been extensively studied, a 40-week report on a related Medifast regimen in 90 individuals with extra weight or obesity showed a substantial decrease in blood pressure. In addition, all Optavia meal plans are planned to have less than 2,300 milligrams of sodium a day, but it is up to you to use low sodium Lean and Green meal alternatives. Numerous health associations recommend drinking fewer than 2,300 mg of sodium a day, including the American Heart Association, College of Medicine, and the United States Department of Agriculture (USDA). That's because greater sodium consumption in sensitive populations is correlated with an elevated risk of hypertension and heart failure.

3. It Offers Continuous Support

For each weight-reduction plan, social support is a critical component of progress. The coaching service and community calls from Optavia include built-in motivation and customer assistance. All throughout weight reduction and maintenance plans, Optavia's fitness trainers are available. Specifically, one analysis identified an important association between the amount of Optavia 5&1 Strategy coaching sessions and enhanced weight loss. In addition, evidence shows that long-term weight management can be facilitated by obtaining a health coach or therapist. Coaching and community help is always excellent. Optavia provides coaching assistance and internet forums, video calls, and group meetings on a weekly basis. Training can be completely virtual, both digitally and by phone, but Optavia has a collection of coaches identified by area if you want to speak with a trainer in person.

4. Achieves Fast Weight Loss

In order to sustain their weight, most stable individuals consume about 1600 to 3000 calories a day. For certain individuals, reducing the amount to as little as 800 calories effectively ensures weight reduction. The 5 & 1 strategy of Optavia is meant for accelerated weight loss, making it a strong choice for those with a legitimate excuse to easily shed pounds.

5. It Removes Guesswork

Some people learn that the most daunting aspect of healthy eating is the emotional work needed to find out what to consume every day or even every dinner. Optavia alleviates the burden of meal preparation and "decision fatigue" by delivering "Fuelings" and "lean and green" menu suggestions to users for clear-cut accepted foods.

Cons Of Optavia Diet Plan

Optavia's plan still has some possible downsides, particularly if you are concerned about the expense, flexibility, and choice.

1. High Monthly Cost

The price of Optavia may be a barrier to targeted clients. For 119 servings (approximately three weeks of diet foods), the 5 & 1 option varies in price from $350 to $425. When you weigh the expense of the initiative, don't neglect to take into consideration the ingredients that you may need to get to cook your "lean and green" recipes.

2. Includes Processed Food

While the "Fuelings" of Optavia are designed with compatible ingredients, they are also clearly processed items, which for certain consumers can be a turn-off. A nutrition study has demonstrated that consuming a lot of processed food may have adverse consequences on one's wellbeing, so there may be a downside to this component of the diet plan.

3. It Might Not Be Sustainable Weight Loss

Losing weight is simple with the Optavia Diet, but holding it off is a struggle. One challenge common to those on a diet is deciding how to sustain weight reduction after the regimen is over. For Optavia's program, the very same applies. When people return to consuming normal meals rather than meal substitutes from the program, they will notice that they easily recover the pounds they dropped.

Our bodies are really wise, and by heading into starvation mode, they can adapt to your low-calorie diet over time. You will begin to draw into your lean body mass instead of fat when you drop more than two pounds a week. And, even if you plan to fuel every few hours, you might still be hungry during the diet.

4. Calorie Restriction Effects

While Optavia's diet plan stresses regularly eating during the day, only 110 calories are produced by each of its "fuels." "Lean and green" recipes are limited in calories as well. If you usually consume fewer calories, you will find that the diet leaves you dissatisfied and unsatisfied. You can still feel drained and sometimes irritable more quickly.

Optavia's highly low-calorie nature comes with dangers. Although weight reduction is not often as easy as calories-in compared to calories-out, 1,100 calories is a major cut from what most of us eat on a normal day, so you are likely to lose weight easily, particularly with the 5 & 1 diet. You will show effects in the beginning if you consume low-calorie food.

5. Isolation And Boredom At Mealtimes

The social implications of cooking and consuming food will conflict with Optavia's dependency on meal replacements. At home dinnertime or while eating out with mates, users can find it uncomfortable or frustrating to get a shake or treat. A meal replacement plan can be a chance to strategize your weekly menus, but with the monotony, it can pose a burden. Besides, while the buddies are reaching happy hour, there's no doubt it's hard to pick a granola bar.

6. Food Reactions

Optavia diet is a high-protein diet with a protein filling up to more than a third of the daily calories. The refined, powdered form, however, may contribute to some unpleasant implications. You can feel your stomach being distended and have other unpleasant gastrointestinal repercussions with the amino acids and other certain additives, leaving you better off with a smoothie with unflavored plain yogurt for your daily protein requirement. Also, for health and safety, the Food and Drug Administration actually does not control nutritionally supplementary products like such as shakes and protein bars the same as it does with food. The 'blends' of powders and proteins definitely contain certain undesirable additives or may interfere with a medicine you might be taking.

Chapter 3: Optimal Weight 5 &1 Plan

The clinically validated Optimum Weight 5 & 1 Plan advises you to consume six balanced meals per day, an essential task that allows you to retain a healthier weight. It's quick, hassle-free, easy to execute, and once every two to three hours is centered on the good practice of eating six small meals a day. You will start making changes right away with the help of your OPTAVIA trainer and their support network.

OPTAVIA Fuelings offer five of your regular meals. Like beverages, soups, bars, hot drinks, healthy options, cookies, pretzels, pancakes, and brownies, pick from more than 50 tasty, easy, nutritionally compatible, scientifically formulated fuels. Each Fueling is developed by the food sciences team and perfected by their Registered Dietitians and fitness team with an almost equivalent nutritional profile.

Scientifically designed with the right mix of carbohydrates, protein, and fat, each OPTAVIA Fueling helps foster a gentle yet successful level of fat burning. Every Fueling provides high-quality, full protein that helps sustain lean body mass. OPTAVIA Fueling is a clean mark that does not include fake coloring, additives, or sweeteners. As part of a good diet and healthier lifestyle, Each Fueling provides GanedenBC30 ® probiotic cultures that help improve digestive health. At the outset, your OPTAVIA Trainer will help you pick your Fuelings, and you can soon find your own choices. You'll discover another great practice, in addition to five Fuelings every day, how to create a Lean & Green meal for both you and your family. You're going to start understanding what a balanced diet feels like, and balanced food can

quickly become part of the routine.

3.1 Extras For The Optimum Weight 5 & 1 Plan

The following are all the extras that you can have in your 5 & 1 weight loss plan.

1. Optional Snacks

You can select one of these optional snacks daily in combination with the five Fuelings and one Lean &

Green dinner. Speak to your OPTAVIA Coach regarding optional snacks that are plan-approved, including:

- OPTAVIA's Puffed Chips or Popcorn

- Three stalks of celery

- One sugar-free fruit-flavored Popsicle

- 1/2 cup of sugar-free jelly serving, like Jell

- Up to 3 sugar-free chewing gum or mints

- Two spears of dill pickles

- 1/2 oz. Nuts: walnuts (7 halves), almonds (10 whole), or pistachios (20 whole). Be conscious that nuts are indeed a rich source of good fat and extra calories. Pick this available snack sparingly.

2. Flavors of Home ®

The Flavors of Home line from Optavia is the best solution to dinner when life is just too crazy for cooking. Each Home Flavors alternative is a full

OPTAVIA Program Lean & Green meal with the correct amounts of lean meat, veggies, and fat. Nutritious, tasty recipes that taste natural but take just minutes to create are produced for each meal.

3. Purposeful Hydration ®

One positive behavior truly contributes to another with OPTAVIA, and staying hydrated is just as crucial to ensuring lasting improvement as eating healthy. OPTAVIA Purposeful Hydration offers core functional advantages that render hydration an easy, delicious activity.

- **Start Strong** comprises quite enough Vitamin C as six tangerines, which also helps ensure a healthy immune function.

- **B Active** is an outstanding source of all B vitamins, helping to promote the production of cellular resources.

- **Replenish** tends to replace the major electrolytes lost in normal activity and during the busy day.

(**Note**: Coaches suggest consuming 64 ml of fluid per day. Before adjusting the quantity of water you consume, check with the healthcare professional since it will impact some health problems and treatments).

4. Optional Condiments

To add taste and richness to your recipes, include condiments; just consider that they lead to the total amount of carbohydrates. For optimum outcomes, we suggest consulting product labeling for carbohydrate details and monitoring condiment servings. A serving of condiments must provide no upwards of 1 g per serving of carbohydrates. On the Optimal Weight 5 & 1 Program, you will enjoy two to 3 condiment servings a day.

Examples:

- Half a teaspoon of salt

- Some dried herbs and spices are half teaspoon, BBQ sauce, catsup, vinegar, Worcestershire sauce, or cocktail sauce.

- One tablespoon of chopped onion, soy sauce, salsa, yellow mustard, soy milk, or other fat-free milk.

- Two teaspoons of any healthy juice of lemon or lime

- Two teaspoons (you can use Torani, DaVinci, Inc., Walden Farms, etc.) of sugar-free flavor syrup

- One sachet no-calorie sugar substitute

- One cup of cool, sugar-free plain or sugar-free flavored vanilla almond or hazelnut milk.

Chapter 4: Lean & Green Meals

Depending on the options for lean protein, a Lean & Green meal contains 5 to 7 oz. of some healthy lean protein that is thoroughly cooked along with three serves of veggies that are specifically non-starchy and low-crab in nature and two parts of the good fats. Any time of day, eat your Lean & Green food, however fits better with your schedule.

Using the below Lean & Green Meal Nutrient Criteria to better lead your decisions, whether you are eating out or measuring your intake:

Healthy Fats

Integrate up to two portions of good fats with your Lean & Green meal every day. Good fats are essential because they help to digest vitamins such as A, D, E, and K from your body. They even support the proper functioning of the gallbladder. There should be 5 grams of overall fat and fewer than 5 g of carbohydrates in a serving of good fat. Below, you will find a bunch of healthy fat options.

4.1 The "Lean" Part Of Your Lean & Green Meal

Below are a few of the helpful tips for choosing your "Lean" protein. These portion size guidelines are for cooked weight only, not raw.

- Choose grilled, roasted, steamed, or poached meat, not fried.

- Prefer to eat at least two portions of fish (salmon, cod, sardines, trout, or herring) high in omega-3 fatty acids a week.

- Feel free to use choices like tofu and kimchi that are meat-free.

Please check the Vegetarian Information Sheet or email Nutrition Help (NutritionSupport@OPTAVIA.com) for a full list of meatless choices.

Choose from the collection that will be listed below the required single serving of any meat. We've sorted protein into the leanest, leaner, and lean choices. For the Ideal Weight 5 & 1 Program, all methods are suitable; this merely lets you make better food decisions. You will use the following nutritional details for any protein alternative, not on the list, to decide whether it is suitable for the OPTAVIA system.

Lean & Green Meal Nutritional Criteria

- Calories = 250-400 Kcal
- 20 grams of carbohydrates (preferably < 15 g)
- Greater than or equal to 25 grams of Protein
- 10-20 grams of fat

"Lean" Part of the Lean & Green Meal

- 180-300 Calories

- Carbohydrates <= 15 g

- Protein >= 25 g

- For fat, refer to the groups of specific proteins below

Leanest Protein Options

- Pick 5 oz. Cooked part of 10 g - 20 g of total fat with no extra Good Fat portion.

- Fish: trout, salmon (Bluefin steak), halibut, mackerel, farmed catfish

- Lean beef: roast, barbecue, minced

- Mutton

- Pork chop or tenderloin pork

- Turkey meatballs or other protein which is approximately 85%-94% lean meat

- Dark meat: poultry or turkey

Your choices for meat-free protein are:

- 15 oz. extra firm or medium tofu

- 3 complete eggs (up to 2 days a week)

- Four ounces of lowered-fat or skim cheese (3-6 g fat per oz.) or 1 cup shredded.

- 8 oz. • (1 cup) Ricotta part-skim cheese (2-3 g of fat per oz.)

- Five ounces. of tempeh

Leanest Protein Options

- Pick 7 oz. Cooked section with 0-4 g net fat and 2 Good fat portions incorporated.

- Fish: flounder, shrimp, salmon, grouper, orange roughy, haddock, tuna, wild catfish (fresh meat or canned in brine)

- Shellfish: lobster, shrimp, scallops, crabs

- Game meat: moose, cows, deer

- Ground turkey or other protein: roughly 98 percent lean meat

Your choices for meat-free protein are:

- 14 whites of egg

- 2 cups of fresh egg whites or fresh egg replacer

- Five oz. of seitan

- 1 and a half cups (12 ounces) 1% cottage cheese

- 12 ounces of Non-fat regular Greek yogurt (about 15 g carb per 12 ounces) (0 percent)

Leaner Protein Options

- Pick 6 oz. Cooked part with 5 to 9 g of fat content and one good fat serving attached.

- Turkey meatballs or any other protein: 95%-97% lean meat

- Turkey: Light meat

- Poultry: breast or white meat, stripped of skin

- Fish: salmon, shrimp, halibut

Your choices for meat-free protein are:

- 2 entire eggs and one cup of liquid egg replacement

- 1 1/2 cups (12 ounces) 2% cottage cheese

- 12 ounces of any good low-fat (2%) regular Greek yogurt (which is approximately 15 g carb per 12 oz.)

- 2 full eggs and four whites of eggs

Healthy Fat Servings

Around 5 g of fat and much less than 5 g of carbs can be included in a good fat portion. Attach 0 2 regular Good Fat Portions depending on the Lean Options:

- 1 teaspoon of oil (any sort)

- 1 tablespoon of normal, low-carb dressing for the salad

- 2 teaspoons lessened-fat, low-carb dressing for a salad

- 5-10 green or black olives

- 1 1/2 oz. Avocado

- 1/3 oz. Simple food items, such as peanuts, pistachios, or almonds

- 1 tablespoon of regular seeds, like chia seeds, flaxseed, pumpkin seeds, or sesame seeds

- Standard butter, ghee, or mayo for 1/2 tablespoons

(Note: See the Condiment & Healthy Fat page site for a full list of good fat choices).

4.2 The "Green" Part Of Your Lean & Green Meal

For each one of the Lean & Green meals, pick three meals from the Green list of options below. We also grouped the choices for vegetables into higher, moderate, and lower amounts of carbohydrates. On the Optimum Weight 5 & 1 Schedule, each is acceptable; the guide lets you make better decisions regarding food.

From the Green Choices List, select three servings:

- One portion = 1/2 cup of vegetables with less than or equal to 25 calories and less than or just about 5 g of carbohydrate (until otherwise indicated).

(NOTE: All vegetables encourage healthier eating. However, we omit the highest possible carb veggies (such as broccoli, maize, peas, potatoes, onions, asparagus, and green beans) in the Optimum Weight 5 & 1 Strategy to boost the outcomes. We urge you to use more veggies for long-term wellbeing after you've reached your healthier weight).

Lower Carbohydrate Greens

- One cup: collard (fresh/raw), endive, cabbage, mustard greens, lettuce (fresh/raw), spring mix, watercress, scallions (raw), green leaf, zucchini squash, broccoli, romaine.

- Half a cup of Arugula, cucumbers, celery, radishes, jalapeño (raw), sprouts (mung bean, alfalfa), white mushrooms, escarole, Swiss chard (raw), turnip greens, nopales, bokchoy (cooked).

Moderate Carbohydrate Greens

- Half a cup: asparagus, eggplant, summer squash (zucchini or scallop), broccoli, lettuce, roasted spinach, fennel seed, portabella mushrooms, cauliflower, etc.

- **Higher Carbohydrate Greens**

- Half a cup: Turnips, cooked Swiss chard, cooked chayote squash, cooked mustard or collard leaves, red cabbage, broccoli, jicama, cooked squash, cooked green or wax beans, cooked kohlrabi, cooked leeks, cooked peppers, raw scallions, palm hearts, cooked summer squash (crookneck), cooked tomatoes, okra, cooked spaghetti squash.

4.3 Lean & Green Meals When You're Dining

Out

You have straightforward instructions for what, where, and how much to consume when you're on the Optavia 5 & 1 Program. So what about going out while you are on your plan? With balanced Lean & Green Meals, or healthy choices for the Transition and Maintenance periods, you will remain on track almost everywhere you go. Just a bit of preparation and innovation is what it requires. Many restaurants have options that, with a bit of change, are consistent with the system or can be. The vital thing to remember is that asking your waiter questions regarding the "customization" of your meal is all correct. Most places will be more than willing to satisfy specific needs and can provide free, or with a minor extra fee, alternative replacements.

Check the guidelines for the appropriate beverages. Simple water is still suitable; use a lime slice and ice or your chosen Flavor Infuser to spruce it up. Stick to drinks that are calorie-free, such as diet drinks, sugar-free tea, coffee, fizzy water, or seltzer that is salt-free.

OPTAVIA would not encourage the consumption of alcohol in people who are in the program's weight loss phase, particularly if you have diabetes. Alcohol not only contributes empty calories but facilitates exhaustion and may reduce willpower, reducing one's approach to the desire to order bad foods. In comparison, the impact of alcohol on those adopting a reduced-calorie food program will be felt more easily and can raise the risk of associated side effects with alcohol use.

Tips To Stay On Track Before Your Dine Out

1. Be Ready, Be Willing

Good eating will become a common routine once you understand what a balanced diet feels like. You would just be aware of exactly what to do when a sudden dining chance introduces itself.

2. Ask Yourself These Questions:

- What will I do if anyone causes me a tough time making my decisions?

- What will I do if I haven't been to this place before?

- What will I do if they do have my beloved dessert/dish?

You would be well able to cope with them with ease by simply "talking yourself through" the scenarios you are likely to experience at the restaurant. Eating out is fun and hassle-free with just a little planning.

3. Research Menus

Many diners have online menus, and some also print their dishes with nutritional values. If there is no information there and the restaurant is close, try pulling up for an early look. Using the Lean & Green dietary criteria as a reference, make better decisions when nutrition knowledge is available. Taking a look at the deals in advance helps you to take your time and allows safe, conscientious decisions. Without feeling pressured or self-conscious, you'll recognize what to order once you're comfortable. If you can't seem to find one that is perfect for your program phase, inquire! Most restaurants under the Lean & Green meal standards are able to satisfy basic demands for something.

You should feel secure in inquiring about healthier foods, much like you will not think twice before buying anything unique for those with food intolerances or other nutritional requirements. Know, the goal is to feel better regarding your nutritious decisions.

4. Choose Supportive Companions

Often it's just as important to acknowledge who you hang with as where you hang. Make sure your friends are respectful of you and your activities the first few occasions you consume in a diner after beginning the OPTAVIA path. Soon, no matter the business, you'll be relaxed enough to make the correct choices.

Few Other Useful Tips:

When choosing how to get your food prepared, bear in mind that extra calories and fat may be applied to some cooking techniques. To also make sure the diet is lower in calories, get your food cooked with a few of these suggested ways.

- Adhere to the suggested plan, when on the 5 & 1 method, stick to the Lean protein and veggie products list.

- Have a "naked" food for you. This implies with sauces excluded or on the side, seasonings or condiments also absent or served separately.

- While consuming beef, pick fillet, pork belly (tenderloin), or round cut, and often cut the obvious fat out of the beef.

- Stay with soups based on broth. Soups of cream (not Optavia's own soups) seem to be higher in calories and fat.

- The healthiest sauce options are marinara, olive oil, or tomato-based sauces.

- "Low-carb" would not imply "low-calorie" inherently or "low-fat." Make sure to closely read through the review to decide if the item is truly a "low-carb" item and the best dietary choice.

- Select stuff created from whole goods while in maintenance like whole grains like brown rice, pasta, and bread of whole wheat.

Tips To Stay On Track While You're Dining Out

- Hold food portions under regulation.

- Ask for a 'to-go' bag as the meal is brought to your plate; if you get a whopper piece, then place half of the food in there for tomorrow.

- Share side dishes, appetizers, and sweets. Half of a meal means half of the carbs.

- To further slowdown the feeding, bring the spoons down in between chews.

- Concentrate on togetherness instead of food and calories.

- As soon as you stop enjoying a sufficient amount, get your plate cleared.

Fast Food

There is processed food everywhere; it's affordable and easy. Yet others are full of fat, carbohydrates, and kcal as well. To eat a small snack without losing your ideal lifestyle, obey these quick instructions.

- Be mindful that in terms of calories, g of fat, and nutrition, not all natural-sounding greens and toppings are actually healthy. Confirm and inquire often.

- Skip all fried foods, since they appear to be full of saturated (bad) fat.

- Stop consuming soft beverages or juices (although the free refills are tempting) that are sugared with high fructose corn syrup. They are made of hollow calories and lots of sugar.

- Stop "max sizing" the meal or "money sizing." It is not worth it. When it challenges your fitness targets by becoming three or four times more than you would otherwise be getting, compromise.

- Request children's meals that is lighter.

- Don't order meals of a combo. They add additional calories per gram, even if they might be easy, so stay with single products.

If You're On The 5 & 1 Plan (Weight Loss Phase):

- Consume the beef without the bun for burgers or fillet sandwiches.

- Stay with grilled option(no chicken wings or fried chicken), not marinated or crispy.

- Query on the side about toppings, sauces, and condiments.

If You Are In The Phase Of Weight-Maintenance:

- Skip bacon or cheese. Ask for a little bit on the side if you're missing these additions.

- If you choose anything delicious, miss hot chocolate or biscuits and just go for a plate of berries.

- Avoid the "special sauces" or mayonnaise filled with calories, fat, or sugar. The fat and calories in ranch dressing, mustard, ketchup, and peppers are smaller.

- By cutting the top burger bread or lunch roll, create an open-faced burger, but you have less processed white flour.

Indian Cuisine

Indian cuisine is made of herbal spices and healthy vegetables. Here's how to appreciate the subcontinent's distinctive tastes while keeping on board with the Optavia plan.

- Stop ghee-containing foods, which is basically clarified butter.

- Inquire about your meal minus nuts, as they are a part of several South Asian recipes.

- Inquire for side sauces.

- Skip malai food, indicating cream, and makhani food, which are crafted with butter.

- Resist fried foods and "crispy" or "golden" dishes in the term.

- Skip soups or sauces made of high-fat coconut.

If You're On The 5 & 1 Plan (Phase Of Weight Loss):

- consider the following suitable meals for Lean & Green Meal:

- Sabzi, sag, or bharta: cooked vegetable generic words

- Chicken tikka: chicken breast, skin-free chicken bits marinated with seasoning

- Kebab: beef or produce skewered

- Qeema: a minced dish of meat

- Ask to prepare your meat and veg with no or little oil.

If You Are In The Phase Of Weight-Maintenance:

- Usually, entrées are followed by a slice of pita bread and a huge proportion of rice. As your flatbread choice, avoid the rice and request for roti. Instead of white flour, roti is usually produced with whole-wheat flour.

Italian Cuisine

Though tasty and famous, Italian food will test your innovation if you eat clean, with its pasta, rich condiments, noodles, and cheeses (no matter the wine), but it's not unthinkable.

Simply follow these tips:

- Remind the server not to add bread to the plate to prevent any urges. The bulk of Italian baked goods are poor in dietary value, strong in carbs and rich in calories.

- Keep away from cream-based soups and stews, pasta (particularly butter-filled), and fat-filled sauces.

- To lower fat and calories, stop dishes cooked with seeds or nuts.

- As cooking water and soups are typically highly salted, stop applying sodium chloride to your food.

- Skip the delicious and jam-packed calories and fat of Italian sweets and pastries.

- Resist salad with croutons and animal products.

- Pick vegetable-rich dishes.

- Choose meat or fish that is roasted, sautéed, or barbecued, and keep away from options that are breaded, caramelized, or baked in any sort of marinade.

- On the side, pick a sauce. Sauces appear to add a number of additional fat, carbs, fat, and sodium, mostly Alfredo, parmesan, Marsala, pesto, Bolognese, and champagne sauce.

- Just get an appetizer portions or side serving as a meal, together with a salad.

- Choose food to share with a buddy when you start feeding or call for a "to-go" box so you can measure your lunch properly.

- When purchasing a meal, select sauce on the side.

If You're On The 5 & 1 Plan (Phase Of Weight Loss):

- Ask for chicken, pork, smoked salmon, or tuna, and no pasta to your server.

- Serve with tomatoes, caramelized onions, mushrooms, lettuce, peppers, broccoli, and asparagus.

- Order meat without a covering and side gravy.

- Try a salad filled with grilled salmon, shrimp, scallops, or some other lean meat, either without shredded cheese or croutons.

If You Are In The Phase Of Weight-Maintenance:

- If appropriate, order pizza or pasta meals with whole-wheat pasta or whole wheat crust.

- For your pasta or pizza, select low-fat cheese and toppings.

- Say no to all deals for extra cheese.

- For extra taste, go for additional spices or herbs.

- Stock up on soups based on broth, such as split pea soup or Italian wedding soup.

Mexican Cuisine

Although every restaurant is different, several U.S. Mexican restaurants rely on Tex-Mex-style foods cooked or fried in oil with lard, cheese, and sour cream. By adopting these rules, you will experience a fiesta with tasty, balanced tastes:

- Remind your server not to deliver tortilla chips to your table to avoid any snacking urges.

- Order dishes full of protein and vegetables that are lean.

- Quantities of Mexican restaurant food can be massive. Share with a buddy a lunch or avoid eating after you have had a sufficient quantity of food and save the remainder for tomorrow in a "to-go" package.

If You're On The 5 & 1 Plan (Phase Of Weight Loss):

- Few samples of Lean & Green Meal-compatible Mexican restaurant food are:

- Taco salad: Order it without a bowl of cheese, cream cheese, quesadillas, or fried tortilla and with side sauce.

- Meat or vegetarian fajitas should be consumed without tortillas, cheese, sour cream, or guacamole.

- Eat any grilled meat, beef, or fish excluding cheese, tortilla shells, sour cream, or avocados,

- Most dishes come with beans and rice; alternatively, demand for even more veggies.

- Often ask for preparation of your order without the use of additional butter or pork fat.

Chapter 5: Transition And Optimal Health 3 & 3

Plan

In this chapter, we'll discuss the details about your transition phase and the 3 & 3 Plan that follows it once you reach your ideal weight through 5 & 1. We'll discuss your Fuelings, sample meal plan, and your 4-week habits of health journey.

5.1 Transition Phase

Optavia's here to help you adjust to consistent healthier eating once you've reached your optimum weight and have understood what balanced food feels like. The transition process raises your consumption of calories steadily and reintroduces a larger range of foods. The kcal you need to sustain your weight after transformation differs according to your height, weight, gender, age, and level of exercise.

This period of 6 weeks leads to an eventual goal of fewer than 1,550 calories a day. Example meal plans for Transition are accessible online.

Sample Meal Plans For Transition

- 1 week: 850 to 1050 calories

- OPTAVIA Fueling: 5 Fueling per day

- Lean and green meals: 1 meal per day that is homemade

- 1 cup of supplementary vegetables (2 parts)

Breakfast

- OPTAVIA Golden Basic Pancakes

Fueling in the Mid-Morning

- OPTAVIA Sweet Blueberry Biscuit

Lunchtime

- OPTAVIA Cheddar Mac Cheesy Buttermilk with 1 cup of chopped tomato and bell pepper

Fueling for the Mid-Afternoon

- OPTAVIA Zesty Cheddar & Crunchers with Italian Herb

Dinnertime

- Five ounces of Grilled salmon with one and a half cups of asparagus

Fueling for the Evening

- OPTAVIA Fudge Pudding in Chocolate flavor

5.2 The 3 Basic Steps To Your 3 & 3 Journey

You may follow the Optimum Health 3 & 3 Program In three simple steps. These are as follows:

Step 1

Calculate the average consumption of energy (TEE), which is the sum of calories you consume per day. For our cumulative energy consumption chart, visit OPTAVIA.com. The Optimum Health 3 & 3 Strategy is focused on matching your food consumption with the calories you consume, a popular method for keeping a healthier weight. Note, an essential aspect of keeping a healthier weight is to improve fitness as well.

Step2

Based on your TEE, pick your meal schedule. Good eating becomes a common standard because you realize what a balanced diet looks like. A number of meal plans varying from 1,200-2,500 calories have been produced by Optavia's specialist nutrition experts. To see the Optimum Health 3 & 3 Plan Sample Meal Plans paper, check the Program Guides & Information Sheets page on ANSWERS.OPTAVIA.com for more details.

Step 3

Get acquainted with the food groups of the program, which involve fruits, milk, starches, oils, fats, and vegetables. Pick items from the 'Balanced Trade List' as substitutions to add variety. You may make one Free Option a day, too. Any of the 'Healthy Exchange List' food choices are roughly 100 calories and can be provided as a free choice as well. You can find ideas for both safe markets and free choices at *answers.optavia.com.*

Through this plan, you will be able to progress on your journey towards optimum health. When your ideal weight has been reached, keeping the healthy actions you have developed, including feeding the body every two or three hours, is important. Optavia also established the Optimal Health 3 & 3 plan to support you in managing a healthier weight. It emphasizes on nutritionally healthy small meals, such as the Optimal Weight 5 & 1 Plan, consumed per two to three hours, thus combining further food options into the right quantities. Your OPTAVIA trainer will guide you more about the Optimal Health 3 & 3 framework prepared by Optavia's team of certified nutritionists.

Using three Optimal Health Fuels every day and three nutritious meals to adopt the Optimal Health 3 & 3 Program

5.3 Optimal Health Fuelings For 3 & 3 Plan

These Fuelings are:

- Safe from synthetic forms of flavors, colors, and sugar substitutes

- Rich in protein

- Gluten-Free Approved (excluding Cream & Cookies Shake)

- The Kosher Dairy

- Suitable for Vegetarians too

- The 30-day package allows you to move on the journey to better health and well-being with ease. It encompasses:

- Nine packages of the Optimal Health 3 & 3 Fuelings

- One serving from each assortment of the Flavors of Home meal service

- Six packages of the tasty OPTAVIA Snacks

- One package of Essential 1: Flavor Infuser with Antioxidants

- One Bottle of Free OPTAVIA Blender

5.4 Sample Meal Plans For 3 & 3 Plan

1. A 1200 Calories Meal Plan

Breakfast

- You can take ¾ cup ready-made sugar-free granola or oats (1 Starch)

- You can also take 1 cup of any good skim or low-fat milk (1 Dairy)

Mid-Morning Fueling

- You may take the Optimal Health Strawberry Yogurt Bar (1 Optimal Health Fueling)

Lunch

- You can take ½ cup of cooked cauliflower (1 Vegetable)

- You can take 3 ounces of grilled chicken (1 Protein)

- And ¾ cup low-fat yogurt (1 Dairy)

Mid-Afternoon Fueling

- You may take the Optimal Health Strawberry & Banana Smoothie (1 Optimal Health Fueling)

Dinner

- You may take 2 cups of raw spinach (2 Vegetables)

- You may take 1 cup total of cucumbers, mushrooms, and diced tomatoes

- You may take 3 ounces of baked yellowfin tuna (1 Protein)

- You may also take two tablespoons of low-fat salad dressing (1 Fat)

- Finally, take one small apple (1 Fruit)

You also have 1 Free Choice to consume all throughout the day

2. A 1300 Calories Meal Plan

Breakfast

- 1 cup skim or low-fat milk (1 Dairy)

- You can take ¾ cup of ready-made sugar-free cereal (1 Starch)

Mid-Morning Fueling

- Optimal Health Strawberry Yogurt (1 Optimal Health Fueling)

Lunch

- You can take ½ cup of cooked broccoli (1 Vegetable)

- You can take 3 ounces of grilled chicken (1 Protein)

- Take ¾ cup of low-fat yogurt (1 Dairy)

Mid-Afternoon Fueling

- Optimal Health Strawberry & Banana Smoothie (1 Optimal Health Fueling)

Dinner

- You may take 2 cups of raw spinach (2 Vegetables)

- You can take 1 cup total of peppers, diced tomatoes, and mushrooms

- You may take 3 ounces of baked yellowfin tuna (1 Protein)

- You may take two tablespoons of low-fat salad dressing (1 Fat)

- One small apple (1 Fruit)

Evening Fueling

- OPTAVIA Essential Sweet Blueberry Biscuit (1 OPTAVIA Fueling)

You also have 1 Free Choice to consume all throughout the day

3. A 1400 Calories Mel Plan

Breakfast

- 1 cup skim or low-fat milk (1 Dairy)

- You can take ¾ cup of ready-made sugar-free cereal (1 Starch)

- You can take one and ¼ cup of whole strawberries (1 Fruit)

Mid-Morning Fueling

- Optimal Health Strawberry Yogurt (1 Optimal Health Fueling)

Lunch

- You can take ½ cup of cooked broccoli (1 Vegetable)

- You can take 3 ounces of grilled chicken (1 Protein)

- You can take ¾ cup of low-fat yogurt (1 Dairy)

Mid-Afternoon Fueling

- Optimal Health Strawberry & Banana Smoothie (1 Optimal Health Fueling)

Dinner

- You can take 2 cups of raw spinach (2 Vegetables)

- You can take 1 cup total of peppers, diced tomatoes, and mushrooms

- You can take 3 ounces of baked yellowfin tuna (1 Protein)

- You can take 2 tablespoons of low-fat salad dressing (2 Fat)

- You can take 8 large black olives

- You can take 1 small apple (1 Fruit)

Evening Fueling

- OPTAVIA Essential Sweet Blueberry Biscuit (1 OPTAVIA Fueling)

You also have 1 Free Choice to consume all throughout the day

4. A 1700 Calories Meal Plan

Breakfast

- 1 cup skim or low-fat milk (1 Dairy)

- You can take ¾ cup of ready-made sugar-free cereal (1 Starch)

- You can take 1 and ¼ cup of whole strawberries (1 Fruit)

Mid-Morning Fueling

- Optimal Health Strawberry Yogurt (1 Optimal Health Fueling)

Lunch

- You can take ½ of cup fully cooked broccoli (1 Vegetable)

- You can take 4 ounces of grilled chicken (1 Protein)

- You can take ¾ cup of low-fat yogurt (1 Dairy)

- You can take 1 slice of whole-wheat, brown bread (1 Starch)

Mid-Afternoon Fueling

- Optimal Health Strawberry & Banana Smoothie (1 Optimal Health Fueling)

Dinner

- You can take 2 cups of raw spinach (2 Vegetables)

- You can take 1 cup total of peppers, mushrooms, and diced tomatoes

- You can take 4 ounces of baked yellowfin tuna (1 Protein)

- You can take 2 tablespoons of low-fat salad dressing (2 Fat)

- You can take 8 large black olives

- You can take 1 small apple (1 Fruit)

- Finally, you can also take 1 cup of any good quality skim or low-fat milk (1 Dairy)

Evening Fueling

- Optimal Health Cream and Cookie Blend Shake (1 OPTAVIA Fueling)

You also have 1 Free Choice to consume all throughout the day

5. 4. A 2200 Calories Meal Plan

Breakfast

- 1 cup skim or low-fat milk (1 Dairy)

- You can take ¾ cup of ready-made sugar-free cereal (1 Starch)

- You can take 1 and ¼ cup of whole strawberries (1 Fruit)

Mid-Morning Fueling

- You can take Optimal Health Strawberry Yogurt (1 Optimal Health Fueling)

Lunch

- You can take ½ of cup fully cooked broccoli and cauliflower (1 Vegetable)

- You can take 6 ounces of grilled chicken (1 Protein)

- You can take ¾ cup of low-fat yogurt (1 Dairy)

- You can take 1 slice of whole-wheat, brown bread (1 Starch)

- You can take 1 teaspoon of extra virgin olive oil (1 Fat)

- You can also take 1/2 cup of canned sliced peas that come submerged in juice (1 Fruit)

Mid-Afternoon Fueling

- Optimal Health Banana & Strawberry Shake (1 Optimal Health Fueling)

Dinner

- You can take 2 cups of raw spinach (2 Vegetables)

- You can take 1 cup total of peppers, mushrooms, and diced tomatoes

- You can take 6 ounces of baked yellowfin tuna (1 Protein)

- You can take 2 tablespoons of low-fat salad dressing (2 Fat)

- You can take 8 large black olives

- You can take 1 small apple (1 Fruit)

- Finally, you can also take 1 cup of any good quality skim or low-fat milk (1 Dairy)

- You can take 1 teaspoon of trans-fat-free margarine

- 1/2 cup baked sweet potato (1 Starch)

Evening Fueling

- Optimal Health Cream and Cookie Smoothie (1

OPTAVIA Fueling)

You also have 1 Free Choice to consume all throughout the day

5.5 Your 4-Week Habits Of Health Journey

Let's start the habits of health journey alongside healthy eating. It involves four tiny healthy habits incorporated into your lifestyle gradually, with each one being added every week across a four-week period. Let's have a look.

Week 1: Habits Of Clean Eating And Hydration

(Health microHabit 1: Consume one additional glass of water per day).

Begin the Program for Optimum Weight 5 & 1 and consume 6 tiny meals a day. And consume one more glass of water a day than you do at present. If in the afternoon, with a snack or in the morning, a major gain would be only one additional drink. Drinking plenty of water is important for well-being and tends to combat cravings for food. Focus on consuming an extra glass of water per day, both now and this week. OPTAVIA Purposeful Hydration often aims to render a tasty, easy routine of hydration and gives important practical advantages. Utilize the Habits of health mobile application to monitor your liquid intake and Fuelings since day 1.

Week 2: Mindfulness

By having just one extra glass of water every day before you hit eight glasses (64 ounces), maintain your week 1 microHabit of Wellness. Notice the quantity of water you get in your record every day or by using the Health Habits Application.

(Health microHabit 2: Compose one sentence a day in your OPTAVIA 30 log).

You will continue to exercise mindfulness when the progress starts with balanced fuels. Focus about a moment per day when you had an urge and how you dealt with it, or journal about an achievement. One sentence is what it involves. Mindfulness allows you to take actions that take you further towards excellence. On your OPTAVIA path, introducing this routine into your everyday life would give you an essential archive of your feelings and emotions.

Week 3: Evolve With Habits Of Good Sleep

Oh, kudos! You've been here for two weeks! You are consuming water and writing every day and are well on the way to introducing new lifestyle patterns into everyday life. The theme this week is good sleep. Rest is an integral component of good well-being but is sometimes neglected. It will alleviate discomfort, decrease food cravings, avoid overeating, and enhance performance by having seven to nine hours of tranquil nighttime sleep. Those are a couple of fantastic benefits.

(MicroHabit of Health 3: After 12 noon per day, consume one fewer cup of coffee, beverage, or another form of caffeine).

Your latest microHabit of Wellness is to consume one fewer cup of coffee, tea, or other forms of caffeine after noon every day to develop Healthier Sleep and energy efficiency Habits that can maintain a healthier weight. According to the FDA, about 300 milligrams (mg) of caffeine a day is consumed by the typical American, equal to three shots of espresso or seven cans of soda. If you get rid of caffeine after midday, you're more inclined to have a relaxing night's sleep. In addition, it could render you more susceptible to caffeine and hold you much more alert at night by adopting a reduced-calorie food program.

Week 4: Develop The Habits Of Healthy Movement

Strenuous exercise can do far more damage than good, particularly when you're not prepared. Eating nutritious fuels every two or three hours, consuming enough liquids, journal writing, sleeping well through having less coffee, and becoming mindful create a difference throughout your life. The lifestyle patterns you have already incorporated. Now, once again, with this microHabit of Wellness, you are beginning to be more active.

(Health 4 microHabit: Stand for an additional two minutes per day).

Standing up for your latest Television show or when reading a book is your fresh microHabit of Wellness for the week. When you steady your stance, standing stimulates nearly every muscle in the body. It sounds insignificant, but sitting down less is one of the greatest health tips in years, so an additional 2 minutes of standing per day is a fine idea! Share with your friends and family this exercise to bring further activity into their lifestyles.

Conclusion

After you've read the whole book, let's just recap a bit of everything we've covered so far. The Optavia diet is a series of three programs, two of which concentrate on losing weight and one that is perfect for managing weight. In order to promote weight reduction, the programs are rich in protein and lower in carbs and calories. Each plan requires that you consume at least half of your food in the form of Optavia pre-packaged food. Since the menu asks for carbohydrates, protein, and fat to be ingested, it is, therefore, a reasonably healthy diet in terms of consuming food groups.

As effective as this meal plan is, there are some risks that have also been discussed nonetheless. A far as weight reduction goes, experts agree that while Optavia can benefit its users because it's lower in calories, for the better, it's unlikely to significantly change your eating habits. You're more prone to regain the weight back once you quit your regimen. So, if, as a result of having gone through the plan, a person ends up modifying their eating patterns to eliminate certain unhealthy foods and maintains a healthy weight, it would be an independent beneficial element coming out of this diet– like the cherry on top.

In addition, experts note that this model might not provide sufficient calories to satisfy the needs of your body. So, do consider consulting with a certified nutritionist if you are intrigued in doing it, which will make sure that you stay well-fed and healthy while you work to achieve your target weight.

So, after all of it is said and done, here's a final word for you. We all know how hard life is for people who are overweight. And if you've read this book and have come this far, you must be dealing with a weight problem. At this moment of your journey, it is crucial for you to recognize that you've overcome the hardest task, i.e., the first dreadful step towards health and wellbeing. Please remember that this alone is a commendable feat. And whoever survives the first step can definitely survive the rest and come out of the other side thinner, stronger, wiser, happier, and overall better.

If you need motivation or if you doubt yourself before joining the amazing Optavia Community, rest assured that this is the right thing to do for your health and wellness. The Optavia coaches are always there for you to support you, guide you, and streamline your journey towards personal growth. Never be shy to reach out to them if you need any kind of help.

Do not treat it as a "diet," because clean eating is supposed to be a lifestyle and permanent change and not just a trend. Having said that, forgive yourself if you ever make a mistake along the way. Remember, the journey of a thousand miles still begins with just a single step indeed. So, stand tall, be confident, and just go ahead each day with your ideal vision of yourself in your mind moving a bit closer to your goals every day.